JACQUES LEVRON

CHATEAUX
OF
THE LOIRE

94 black and white, and colour photographs
and map of the châteaux.

Translated by M.-Th. Olano and Ian Robertson

ARTHAUD

In the same collection :

The sights of Carcassonne
Chartres and its cathedral
Chateaux of the Ile-de-France
The sights of Mont-Saint-Michel
Paris
Versailles

On the jacket:
Azay-le-Rideau, from the air (Air photographer Roger Henrard)
The pagoda of Chanteloup and Chinon and the river Vienne
(Henry Paillasson, Editions Arthaud)

CHATEAUX OF THE LOIRE

The Loire châteaux, old castles or luxurious country seats, are not only a perfect expression of great periods of architecture, but are at the same time a reflection of great eras in the French monarchy. And, since Ronsard and Du Bellay, the light of the Loire has shone unceasingly. It represents the very symbol of charm itself, a standard by which all things, in France, were ever gauged in the eyes of strangers. Jacques Levron here describes the changes their glorious features have undergone. By day or night, they appear in an enchanted form, which binds contemporary France to her remote and legendary past.

Amboise	**Chinon**	**Montsoreau**
Angers	**Fontevrault**	**Orléans**
Azay-le-Rideau	**Fougères**	**Le Plessis-Bourré**
Beaugency	**Gien**	**Le Plessis-Macé**
Beauregard	**Langeais**	**Saumur**
Bellegarde	**Loches**	**Serrant**
Blois	**Le Lude**	**Sully**
Brissac	**Luynes**	**Talcy**
Chambord	**Ménars**	**Tours**
Chaumont	**Montgeoffroy**	**Ussé**
Chenonceaux	**Montrésor**	**Valençay**
Cheverny	**Montreuil-Bellay**	**Villandry**

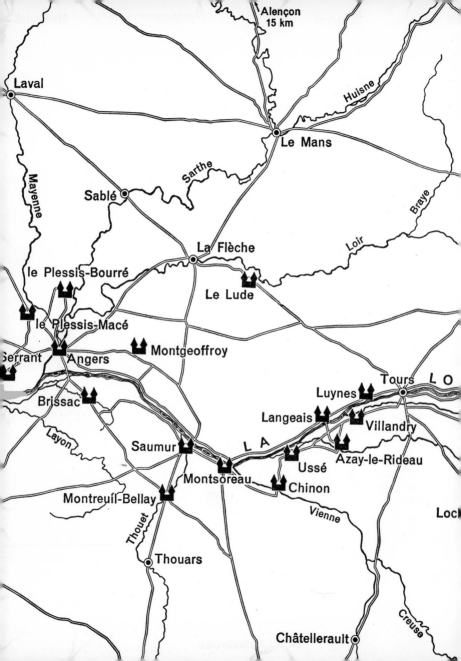

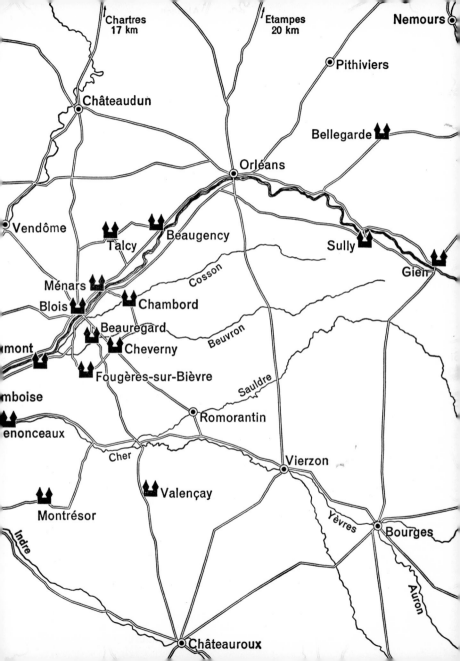

Chartres
17 km

Etampes
20 km

Nemours

Pithiviers

Châteaudun

Bellegarde

Orléans

Vendôme

Talcy

Beaugency

Sully

Gien

Cosson

Ménars

Blois

Chambord

Beauregard

Beuvron

mont

Cheverny

Fougères-sur-Bièvre

Sauldre

mboise

Romorantin

enonceaux

Cher

Vierzon

Valençay

Yèvres

Montrésor

Bourges

Indre

Auron

Châteauroux

INTRODUCTION

FRENCH CHATEAUX

France is a country of châteaux. The long persistence of the seignorial regime, characteristic of an agrarian structure until the Revolution of 1789, partially explains their abundance. Feudal fortresses of Auvergne, of Alsace, country houses of Périgord, Norman manor houses, elegant residences of the Ile de France, each French province offers thus evidence of its past to the visitor.

Nevertheless, amongst all these regions, the Loire Valley seems particularly privileged, and unquestionably those châteaux which are washed by the royal river, between Gien and Ancenis, enjoy universal fame. What was the origin of this celebrity ? Is it to be attributed to the infatuation of certain romantic writers, who chose to frame their works with these châteaux, up to then forgotten ? Balzac, Vigny, and above all Dumas certainly contributed to make the Châteaux of the Loire known. Strangers to this region also took interest in them, and Stendhal noticed that the English had established a preference for Tours as a place where they might improve their knowledge of the French language. Moreover the relative proximity of Paris, and the effects of cleverly managed tourist propaganda for almost a century, have undoubtedly increased the popularity of these châteaux.

But in fact none of these causes would be enough was it not for the fact that this country has seen a prodigious number of buildings grown on her soil; one can count about forty, amongst the most important, to which twenty or so lesser known can be added. No other region can pride itself on having such wealth, and especially within such a small area, for in Touraine they follow each other without interruption. Just as you leave the postern of one, the pointed towers of another are seen in profile at a bend in the road. That the châteaux of the Loire are well known we can understand, but why their abundance ?

THE LOIRE COUNTRY

Firstly the attraction exercised by the Loire country itself : "A huge museum, replete with history and anecdote, so seems this region to the tourist", writes M. Faucher. "The variety of its natural scenery has helped. The valleys and their approaches have become the scene of an intense life, with culture, industry and commerce in harmonious coexistence". It is true that the geological nature of the ground has aided its settlement. The mildness of the climate tempered by the breath of the west winds, the richness of the fertile soil, the peaceful stability of its productions have given the people of the Loire a certain affluence. It is good to live in Touraine and Anjou. One then understands why in this land where beats the heart of France, men have willingly chosen to make their home.

And firstly the kings : the history of these provinces is intimately tied to that of the monarchy. The Orléanais is, almost as much as the Ile de France, the cradle of the Capetian race. When the capital of France was menaced or occupied, it was at Orléans, or Tours that the government found refuge. The Valois in the fifteenth and sixteenth centuries had a liking for this valley where Charles VII, still dauphin, had found help and protection. Louis XI preferred Plessis, Charles VIII Amboise, Francois I Chambord, and one can multiply these examples. Castles have often been called the backcloth of history; never has this been more justified than by those of the Loire.

But the taste of kings was followed by that of their servants. A good courtier should not live far from his master, which is why some châteaux were reconstructed or embellished by families devoted to the king : Jean Bourré at Langeais, Bohier at Chenonceaux, Berthelot at Azay-le-Rideau and many others. That attraction for the valley continued until the middle of the seventeenth century. More rare are the châteaux built during the later period, although Ménars was fitted up during the eighteenth century, while Montgeoffroy dates from the reign of Louis XVI.

Well-stocked forests permitted the pleasures of the chase — Chambord is on the skirts of the Sologne — the people were friendly and, one must not forget, there was ease of access : these provinces which border the Loire are more varied than is often thought, and there are differences in character between the Orléanais, the Tourangeaux or the Angevins, but they are united by the lazy or troubled stream of the great river, once furrowed by boats which plied with merchandise and travellers.

The Loire has ceased to be navigable except by punts of anglers who patiently wait for fish to break surface. But she continues to serve in joining the provinces and gives the country its geographical unity.

THE DIVERSITY OF CHATEAUX

One would makc a great mistake in imagining the châteaux themselves offer any unity of style or appearance. These châteaux of the Loire are unbelievably different and all periods are represented. One could easily confound châteaux of the Loire with Renaissance châteaux yet nothing is more inexact. Certainly the great period of building extends, at least for the most famous among them, to the sixteenth century. But it is better not to be too summary in one's judgements.

The most ancient vestiges of French military architecture is to be found at the keep of Langeais, which reaches back to the end of the tenth century. The seventeen towers of Angers disclose to our admiration the strength and sturdiness of the thirteenth century fortress, and they constitute one of the most striking examples of the mediaeval citadel. But Loches, Chinon, Vendôme, now uninhabited stone skeletons, also take us back to the Middle Ages. When the Valois settled along the Loire they brought with them more luxury and light to such forbidding dwellings, but even so they were careful not to overlook their defensive characteristics, and as long as danger was likely to threaten the kingdom, the château retained elements essential to its protection, the wall walks, watchtowers, and barbicans. Montsoreau, Langeais or Plessis-Bourré are remarkable in this respect ; elegance makes its appearance, but the structure as a whole is still grim.

One knows that Charles VIII, by bringing workers and artisans from Italy with their modern ideas in design (which was in fact no more than a return to Antiquity) introduced the latter into France. Nevertheless, very slowly, with discretion, the master builders adopted the Renaissance style. The plan of Chambord is still completely traditional. The château of Amboise juxtaposes flamboyant gothic with the new style. According to Edouard Herriot, it was at Chaumont and at Chenonceaux that the Spring of French Renaissance architecture smiled. This blossomed at Blois and Chambord.

There is therefore a remarkable adaptation of Italian art by the French. It has been often stated : the Renaissance was the achievement of princes and they imposed this setting which was then copied elsewhere in the area. There again one must avoid another misconception in thinking that with the sixteenth century the building of the châteaux of the Loire ceased. In spite of the return of the Valois to Paris or Fontainebleau, and the Bourbons installing themselves round the capital, no "blanket" of indifference spread over the valley. Cheverny and Brissac are excellent examples of the Louis XIII style. Serrant was not completed until Louis XIV reign. All the charm of Ménars is due to the Marquise de Pompadour and her brother, the Marquis de Marigny. Under Louis XVI châteaux were still being born, like Montgeoffroy, which was built by the Marshal de Contades less than fifteen years before the Revolution.

The same diversity is found inside these châteaux, some of them possess sumptuous furnishings, tapestries or pictures. The halls of others remain empty, deserted, and nothing is there to distract one from recreating the atmosphere of historic scenes which have there taken place. Several châteaux belong to the State and have been turned into museums. Others are still in the hands of their owners (who are often descendants of their original builders) and the warmth of life has not left them. And then, of course their settings are also varied. One finds some lost in the forest, like Ussé, others, such as Villandry, Chenonceaux or Ménars are adorned with beautiful gardens.

ADVICE TO VISITORS

There is no chance of being bored when visiting the châteaux of the Loire, but even so it must be done at leisure. Nothing is worse than those "tours" during which the traveller is expected to absorb six or seven châteaux at least, in a day, and returns to his hotel in the evening exhausted and confused by all he has seen. One should never look over more than two or three in a day. Take your time, saturate yourself in the scenery, the surroundings, study the history of the château and the plan of its construction and... return to it; for the charm and attraction of such residences is not necessarily obvious at the first visit.

One must observe the châteaux slowly, without haste. Then, little by little, all their beauty, their originality, the similarities which they have to each other, are noticed.

Too often the "tour" of the Loire châteaux generates fatigue. As a relaxation, one should read not only books concerning them, but also the historical and literary works which they have inspired. It is by following the Valley of the Indre that one better appreciates the charm of **Le Lys dans la vallée.** Balzac is still alive at Saché, as is Rabelais at La Devinière. Victor Hugo evoked Blois in famous verses, and René Boylesve has given us a lesson in love in the park, in the garden of Touraine : thus are mingled in our minds our own memories and those of our reading.

And then when night falls, one must go and see the châteaux aglow and listen to the spectacle of "Son et Lumière".

Has it been abused ? It would be rash to say so. One may state on the other hand, that those in the Valley of the Loire (where they were born) are still amongst the best of them. Chambord, the work of the creator of these nocturnal resurrections, leaves the hearer with the feeling that for him alone have these lighting effects and resounding echos been arranged. The lapping of water lends Chenonceaux a delicate charm, which is also given by the ghosts of those ladies who haunted the house.

At Lude, on the Loir, as the foreground of the château is progressively illuminated, all the youth of the town participate in its reconstruction. Everywhere drums beat, swords clash and at the finale of the spectacle it seems as if one is brought back from the distant past.

A visit to the châteaux ought not to make one over-look the towns, which frame them. Great provincial capitals such as Orléans, Tours or Angers, exquisite small towns which have still kept, in spite of new districts and recent buildings, streets bordered with old houses, mansions with elegantly sculptured façades, even villages where the white walls make the bursts of colour of their window boxes seem even more vivid.

The châteaux are renowned, the religious buildings, cathedrals, churches, monasteries, also cause admiration and interest, but one can still, off the beaten track, make discoveries.

How many manors are ignored by the great itineraries. How many sanctuaries are by-passed by tourists' coaches. To the lover of the past, to the archaeologist or artist, the Loire country holds therefore innumerable pleasures. A little patience and much love is all you need.

1. Charles VII. Karl VII. Carlo VII. Carlos VII.

2. Louis XI. Ludwig XI. Luigi XI. Luis XI.

3. Charles VIII. Karl VIII. Carlo VIII. Carlos VIII.

4. Louis XII. Lugwig XII. Luigi XII. Luis XII.

5

Rois, reines, visages de la Loire. Kings and queens : the faces from the Loire. Könige, Königinnen, Profile von den Ufern der Loire. Re, Regine, visi della Loira. Reyes, Reinas, aspectos del Loire.

5. François 1er. Francis I. Franz I. Francesco I. Francisco I°.

7. Anne de Bretagne. Anne of Brittany. Anna di Bretagna. Ana de Bretaña.

6. Claude de France. Claude of France. Claudia di Francia. Claudia de Francia.

8. Catherine de Médicis. Catherine de Medici. Katharina von Medici. Caterina dei Medici. Catalina de Médicis.

9. Henri II. Henry II. Heinrich II. Enrico II. Enrique II.

10. Diane de Poitiers. Diana von Poitiers. Diana di Poitiers. Diana de Poitiers.

11. Charles IX. Karl IX. Carlo IX. Carlos IX.

12. Henri III. Henry III. Heinrich III. Enrico III. Enrique III.

COMMENTARIES

AMBOISE

Built on a rocky spur, the château of Amboise in the Middle Ages guarded the bridgehead and little town. The edifice itself was commenced under Louis XI. But it was Charles VIII — born at Amboise in 1470 — who, after 1492, undertook the great work of reconstruction. This was already well advanced when the king brought back from Italy a group of workmen who exerted their influence principally on its decoration, for it was French masters who conceived the architecture. Charles VIII fractured his skull by hitting it against the door jamb of the Hacquelebac gallery on 7th April, 1498.

Louis XII took over the building later. Francis I finished the wing already commenced. He invited Leonardo da Vinci from Italy who died at Clos Lucé in 1519.

Amboise was the scene of many historical events; in 1560, a Huguenot, La Renaudie, hatched a plot with the intention of seizing Francis III and removing him from the domination of the Guises. The conspiracy was discovered. La Renaudie was killed and his accomplices were hung from the great balcony of the château. It was hardly used after that as a residence by the kings of France. Under Louis XIII it passed to his brother, Gaston d'Orléans. The revolt of Gaston against royal authority, in 1631, resulted in Amboise being deprived of part of its ramparts. The château served as a state prison. Fouquet was shut up there for a few weeks, and later, Lauzun. Louis XV raised the county into a duchy and conferred it upon Choiseul, who, after his disgrace, lived in his nearby estate of Chanteloup. Louis XVI repurchased it to give it to Louis Philippe's grandfather. Under the First Empire, Amboise was handed over to the consul Roger Ducos who pulled down part of the building, which he could not maintain. Abd-el-Kader was held prisoner there between 1848-52. The château belongs now to the state.

The **Chapel of Saint-Hubert,** formerly part of the main building, is a jewel of flamboyant gothic. It was built under Charles VIII. The façade is ornamented by a sculptured tympanum representing the legend of Saint Hubert on the left, and that of St. Christopher on the right. Under a slab lie the supposed remains of Leonardo da Vinci.

The main structure is composed of the **Royal Apartments,** which date from Charles VIII and extend parallel to the Loire, and the **Louis XII wing.** The former are lit by six large double casements connected by a balcony of ancient ironwork, from which were hung, according to tradition, the conspirators of Amboise. Above, the high dormer windows are linked by a pierced stone balustrade. The **State room,** on the first floor, is formed by two naves with ogival vaults.

The **Louis XII wing,** with an additional floor, is of a later style and the attic windows in particular, distinctly belong to the Renaissance.

The surrounding wall, of triangular shape, is propped up by the **tower of the Minimes** and the **Hurtault tower.** The first, with its famous spiral ramp, was practicable for horses, and Charles V and Francis I went up together on horseback. Its decoration, still very gothic at the bottom, increasingly shows Italian influence as it rises. From the top of the wall-walk the view is magnificent.

To the south, the **Hurtault tower,** broader, is purely gothic. It was nearly finished by the time Charles VIII left for Italy.

Of the admirable patterns designed for the gardens by Pacello da Mercogliano only a memory remains.

The town of Amboise possesses several monuments of great interest. You must at least visit the church of Saint Denis (twelfth century) with its statues of the Entombment; the church of Saint Florentine (fifteenth century); the house of Denis Morin (the Town Hall, sixteenth century, much restored) and above all the manor of Clos Lucé which has recently been happily restored. On the outskirts of the forest of Amboise rises the pagoda of Chanteloup.

ANGERS

The first château of Angers was built after 851 following an exchange between the Carolingian count, who administered the town and had lived up till then near the cathedral, and the bishop of the diocese, whose palace stood on the hill which overlooked the Maine. Of this château, nothing remains. Excavations have uncovered an eleventh century chapel (to be seen in the new Museum of the Apocalypse). It is likely that an important work of reconstruction took place during the twelfth century under the Plantagenets. A romanesque door, brought to light in 1947, can be seen.

The château was in a very bad state of repair when Saint Louis, fighting against the Duke of Brittany, Pierre Mauclerc, gave orders for it to be completely rebuilt. Then, between 1230-1238, seventeen massive towers of quarry stone or slate interspersed by a course of sandstone, joined by strong ramparts were built, towers which must always be imagined as being two floors higher than they are, and crowned by watch-turrets. Angers must have been one of the strongest citadels in the kingdom. It was never taken by storm.

In the fifteenth century, Yolande d'Anjou, who defended her lands and the dauphin (the future Charles VII) against the English, repaired the fortifications and had erected (between 1400 and 1409) the elegant flamboyant gothic chapel, which can be admired still.

Born in the château of Angers in 1409, good King René resided there between his adventurous expeditions. He had gardens laid out. He restored principally the beautiful royal rooms of which those in the northern gallery, with gothic vaulting, carry his arms on the keystone.

During the sixteenth century the governor's residence was built against the wall, with its back to the gate called "des Champs", which is still barred by an old wooden portcullis.

That century was almost fatal to the château. During the Religious wars, a captain in the service of the Ligueurs, du Hallot, seized the fortress by a trick. It was with great difficulty that he was ejected, and to avoid such a mishap recurring, Henry III ordered it to be razed to the ground, but the demolition went slowly. Ten years later, the château had only lost one and a half to two floors, and its coping. Peace returned. The governor, with the king's agreement suspended work. From then on a terrace straddled the huge towers.

With the seventeenth century, the château served as a state prison and naturally received Fouquet, arrested by Louis XIV, and escorted by d'Artagnan to his destination. During the Revolution prisoners from the Vendée were piled into its cells. The nineteenth century turned the château into a military school which did not embellish it. Following the bombings of 1944, it has passed over to the administrators of historical monuments who renovated it, restored it to its ancient state and have given it a new lease of life.

Inside the second courtyard, near the keep, an elegant gallery has been built to house and present under the best possible conditions the tapestries of the **Apocalypse.** These hangings ordered by Louis I d'Anjou, were woven between 1375-1380 by the Parisian artist Nicolas Bataille after the sketches of Jean de Bruges. In spite of being cut down they measure 342 feet long. On alternative backgrounds of blues and reds, scenes of the sacred text unwind their allegories. This is both the most ancient and, without doubt, the most sumptuous of French tapestries.

But the different buildings which compose the château hold other tapestries of great merit. One must see the "Angels holding the Instruments of the Passion" (fifteenth century), two Flemish works of the Passion, the "Lady at the Organ" (sixteenth century), Penthesilea, Queen of the Amazons, and several others of more recent date.

AZAY-LE-RIDEAU

Ridel or Rideau, seigneur d'Azay, built in the twelfth century a château which the Indre held in its grip between Tours and Chinon. The fortress was destroyed by Charles VII, dauphin of France, to punish its holder for taking sides amongst his enemies.

The château was re-erected. But the existing building was not begun until 1518. The ground then belonged to Gilles Berthelot, treasurer-general of Finances, and it was left to his wife Philippe Lesbahy, to superintend the work. This was finished before 1527, the year in which the financier fell into disgrace and only escaped the gallows by taking flight. Francis I confiscated the château and stayed there at times. The elegant edifice afterwards belonged to the diplomat

Saint-Gelais. During the seventeenth century, it came into the hands of the first royal groom the count of Béringhem, who received Louis XIV there. It was acquired by the State in 1905.

Azay-le-Rideau is an example of a château which has retained a gothic structure transformed by all the decorative grace of the Renaissance. It still has huge towers, machicolations, and a wall-walk. But the well watered moat which surrounds Azay — the terreplein being done away with, the waters now wash the very foundations of the castle, — now serves as a mirror only. The towers are no longer menacing, and the wall-walk only serves to reach the apartments. In layout, the château is composed of two wings set at right-angles. The architect was certainly inspired by the disposition of the façades of the Francis I wing at Blois. The principal wing was the first built. The ermine of Claude de France and the salamander of Francis I, a delicate attention of the owner to show his regard for his sovereign, date it more than any signature. On the other wing, finished before the disgrace of the financier, are still found the initials of his christian name and that of his wife.

The façades are composed of superimposed floors separated by a double moulding and surmonted by Renaissance dormer-windows. One discovers in some details a Florentine influence. The main entrance, still the most finished, is composed of double windows on two floors, and is topped by two attic windows in finely worked gables. This entrance gives access to a straight staircase, the vault of which is magnificently decorated by coffers ornamented with medallions representing the Kings of France. This stair, in which a formal ascent takes the place of the traditional spiral, is one of the oldest in France (with that of Chenonceaux). An interesting Museum of Renaissance Art embellishes and furnishes the château.

13. Amboise. Façade overlooking the Loire.

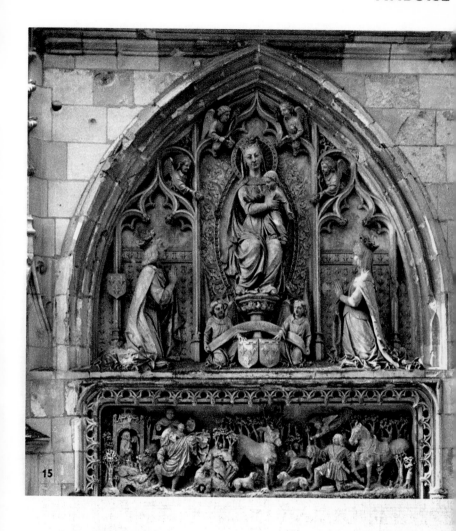

14. La chapelle Saint-Hubert.
The chapel of Saint-Hubert.
Die Saint-Hubert-Kapelle.
La cappella di Sant'Uberto.
La capilla de San Huberto.

15. Haut-relief de la chapelle Saint-Hubert.
High relief in the chapel of Saint-Hubert.
Hochrelief in der Saint-Hubert-Kapelle.
Altorilievo della cappella di Sant'Uberto
Alto relieve de la capilla de San Huberto.

ANGERS

16. Tapisserie de Lurçat. Le chant du monde : l'homme en gloire dans la paix.
Tapestry by Lurçat. The world rejoices : Man in all his glory in peace.
Wandteppich von Lurçat. Das Lied der Welt : Die Herrlichkeit des Menschen
im Frieden.

Arazzo di Lurçat, Il canto del mondo : l'Uomo in maestá nella pace.
Tapices de Lurçat. El canto del mundo : Exaltación del hombre en la paz.

17

18

Tapisseries de l'Apocalypse.
Tapestries of the Apocalypse.
Wandteppiche der Apokalypse.
Arazzi dell'Apocalisse.
Tapices del Apocalipsis.

17. Dieu envoie la nouvelle Cité sainte. God sends the new Jerusalem. Gott sendet die neue Heilige Stadt. Dio porta con sé la nuova città santa. Dios manda la Ciudad Santa.

18. Saint Jean et le fils de l'homme. Saint John and the son of Man. Der Heilige Johannes und der Menschensohn. San Giovanni e il Figlio dell'Uomo. San Juan y el Hijo del Hombre.

19. Babylone détruite est hantée par les démons. Destroyed Babylon is haunted by devils. Das zerstörte Babylon wird von Teufeln heimgesucht. Babilonia distrutta è invasa dai demoni. Babilonia destruída está acosada por los demonios.

19

ANGERS

20

21. Le château et le parc. The chateau and the park. Schloß und Park. Il castello ed il parco. El castillo y parque.

AZAY-LE-RIDEAU

BEAUGENCY

22. Le donjon et la Loire.
The keep and the Loire.
Wachtturm und die Loire.
Il mastio e la Loira.
La torre del homenaje y el Loire.

23. L'hôtel de ville.
The town hall.
Rathaus.
Il municipio.
Ayuntamiento.

22

BEAUREGARD

24. La galerie des portraits.
The portrait gallery.
Die Bildergalerie.
La galleria dei ritratti.
Galería de retratos.

BEAUGENCY

Beaugency does not possess an important castle. But the charm of this little town, which lies peacefully along the river bank is great, and it would be a pity not to stop there.

Caesar's tower — where of course Caesar never set foot — is a tall keep of the eleventh century, when square or rectangular shapes were assumed. The keep of Beaugency is rectangular. It is not less than five floors high and rises 115 feet above the ground. At each corner a buttress is set at right angles. The windows on each floor were enlarged, and some still retain mullions.

The keep of Beaugency suffered much from attack. The town was taken four times by the English during the Hundred Years War. It was Joan of Arc who eventually recaptured it in 1429. The keep was stormed once more during the Religious Wars, and lost its roof. It is today not more than a sumptuous ruin.

The bastard of Louis d'Orléans, the kind Dunois, faithful companion of Joan of Arc, became possessor of Beaugency. The château, which he reconstructed in the fifteenth century and which was finished by his grandson Jean II of Orléans, is an elegant flamboyant gothic dwelling. But it has suffered ample restoration. The polygonal turret is very old. In the interior beautiful woodwork is displayed. One can view an interesting Regional Museum which houses a varied collection of costumes of the Orléans region, some fine furniture and remarkable engravings of the Loire mariners.

The Town Hall dates from the Renaissance. It has also been much restored. Built in 1525, its design has been attributed to members of the Biart family, those architects who worked at Blois and Gaillon. It is an elegant one-story building with a façade ornamented all over by sculptured pilasters, and with medallions framing busts. Between the ground floor and the first floor, which is lit by three large mullioned windows, are sculpted compartments representing the arms of Beaugency, of the house of Longueville and of Jean d'Orléans. Inside is kept beautiful woollen embroidery of the seventeenth century.

The churches of Notre Dame and Saint-Etienne, the tower of Saint-Firmin, and the clock tower should also be visited.

BEAUREGARD

Situated south of Blois, in the commune of Cellettes, the château of Beauregard dominates the course of the Beuvron on the edge of the forest of Russy. In spite of important restorations, it still constitutes a type of Renaissance manor-house, when at its first flowering, although it was not completed until the seventeenth century.

It is in fact composed of two wings set at right angles. The principal one was built about 1545 by Jean du Thier, owner of Beauregard, and a Secretary of State to Henry II, and then continued by his son. Mostly open to the exterior, a gallery occupies the centre of the ground floor. On the first floor, pilasters frame the windows. Finally elegant dormer-windows with sculptured pediments pierce the roof.

The second wing was finished in 1638.

Inside, the first floor gallery is entirely covered with three hundred and sixty-three portraits : kings of France and other famous people. In the lower panellings, little paintings, the work of Jean Mosnier, of Blois, (whom we will meet again at Cheverny) are inserted. The floor is decorated by a curious blue delft tiling which represents an army on the march.

BELLEGARDE

One must move away a little from the Loire valley to visit Bellegarde. This château is in fact situated north-west of Châteauneuf-sur-Loire, between Orléans and Montargis. The feudal fortress was reconstructed during the fourteenth century by the Hospital family; only a rectangular keep with overhanging turrets remains.

After having belonged to the family of Saint Lary, the château passed at the end of the seventeenth century to a nephew of the last member of this family, the Marquis de Montespan, and then to the legitimate son of "la Marquise", Antoine de Parfaillan, marquis and then duc d'Antin.

It was the duc d'Antin who transformed Bellegarde during the eighteenth century. Of all the buildings he erected, only the d'Antin pavilion remains, much changed, the pavilion of the Salamander, which today serves as the Town Hall, and various outhouses. Inside, the municiple council hall is ornamented by a sculptured wainscoting elegantly treated.

The church of Bellegarde dates from the end of the twelfth century and the beginning of the thirteenth. Its Romanesque portal is of great richness.

BLOIS

The House of Blois was from the end of the ninth century one of the most powerful feudal dynasties of France. During the twelfth century its domination spread over all the neighbouring fiefs as far as Champagne. This family faded out in 1241, and in 1397, Louis d'Orléans, brother of Charles VI, acquired the County of Blois. His son Charles, the poet, taken prisoner at Azincourt, was held captive for a quarter of a century. Charles' son Louis, who became king after the death of Charles VIII, established his court at Blois. Francis resided there likewise. His wife Claude de France, had a strong liking for the château, which her husband enlarged and completed.

During the wars between the Ligueurs and the Huguenots, Blois was the scene of great events. From 1576 the States-General of the Kingdom was convoked there, and demanded the inalienability of the royal domain and asserted a limitation of the King's authority. In 1588, another meeting, under the sway of Henri de Guise, Chief of the Ligue, menaced the king himself. Henri III was resolute in disencumbering himself of his rival, and had him assassinated on the 23rd December, 1588. Catherine de Medici, his mother, old and tired, died a few days later.

Under Louis XIII, Marie de Medici — another contrary mother — was constrained by her son to live in the château. It is suggested that she escaped from a window by means of a rope ladder. A few years later, it was the king's brother, Gaston d'Orléans, who was exiled to Blois. He took the opportunity of getting Mansart to lay out grandiose designs intended to transform the château by demolishing the ancient buildings. Of this project, only one wing was accomplished.

During the course of the eighteenth century, the château was deserted for a long period. It was again a question of demolition to reduce the cost imposed on the State. It was left to the military authorities (which did not do it much good), then important restorations were undertaken after 1849. Today part of it serves as a Museum and Library. In 1940 the château was seriously threatened by the fire which devastated that part of the town situated along the Loire. The destruction of two charming houses, those of the duc d'Epernon and the Cardinal d'Amboise, saved it.

The château of Blois is an admirable assembly of buildings, which, dating from the fifteenth to seventeenth century, allow one to follow completely the evolution of French domestic architecture. Each element brings an innovation and yet the continuity of the work remains perceptible.

Of the Middle Ages, all that remains is the tower of Foix (thirteenth century) which dominates the Loire, and the beautiful Hall of State divided into two halves by columns. It is situated in the wing of Charles d'Orléans and was the principal room of the earlier château.

Backing on to the chapel of Saint Calais, built by Louis XII, the wing of Charles d'Orléans (fifteenth century) was demolished on the orders of Gaston d'Orléans. Only a fragment of the gallery remains, of a sober and elegant architecture. The elliptic arches rest on pillars and are topped by a tier of bricks with windows framed with stone.

The Louis XII wing (by which one enters) stretches along the château courtyard, an admirable façade of stone and brick in which Italianism appears only in the details of ornamentation. Two of the windows on the first floor form a balcony which one can see is the prototype of the loggias of Francis I.

The latter built the wing which carries his name, a masterpiece. It must be admitted that the Italian architect Domenico da Cortone, who lived at Blois from 1512 to 1524, could have advised the French architects who were putting up the building between 1515 to 1524.

The great staircase was once enclosed in the centre of the interior façade but was thrown out of line by the construction of Gaston d'Orléans' wing. Between the buttresses, on which figures are sculpted, it opens on to the courtyard by large balustrated balconies. The opposite façade, towards the town, is called the "loggias", because it is formed by two floors of rooms like theatre boxes and a gallery, cut into the thickness of the walls. It recalls the layout of certain Italian palaces.

Lastly the wing of Gaston d'Orléans, built by Mansart, stands at the far end of the courtyard, to the west. Its classical appearance contrasts with the exuberance of the Renaissance. It does not fail for all that either in grandeur or in harmony, with its fluted pilasters, its portico surmounted by a high pediment.

Inside, the Queen's Apartments are fitted up on the first floor of the Francis I wing. They are split up along their length by a wall, the ancient curtain wall of the town against which lean the loggias. One is allowed to visit the dressing room, the bedroom, the oratory and the study (beautifully panelled) of Catherine de Medici, likewise the great gallery of honour. Above are situated the King's Apartments which also include the council room and the guard room. It was at the foot of the bed, in the King's room, that the Duc de Guise fell stabbed by the 45 gentlemen chosen by Henri III to carry out this task.

BRISSAC

An unscrupulous miller who made holes in his customers sacks, such would be, so they say, the origin of the name Brissac (Brêchesac or split bag). Be that as it may, to cover the south side of the capital of Anjou, above the Aubance, the site was well chosen.

A château existed there in the eleventh century. It was rebuilt at the conclusion of the Hundred Years War by Pierre de Brézé, Councillor of Charles VII and Louis XI. From this time date the two huge cylindrical towers, the wall-walk and machicolations, which flank the principal façade. In 1502 the château passed to the de Cossé family. The Wars of Religion caused much damage to the citadel. Charles II de Cossé, whom Henri IV had largely rewarded because he had opened to him the gates of Paris in 1594, undertook its reconstruction. He received the marshal's baton and the county was raised to a duchy in 1611.

Under the direction of Jacques Corbineau the great mass of five floors rose, on which were superimposed the classical orders. A high central pavilion was crowned by a bell tower which was taken down during the Revolution. Niches flank the large semicircular windows of the pavilion (the first three floors) and the two upper floors only have little windows.

The plan must have been grandiose. It was to remain unfinished, which explains why the pavilion was never flanked by the wing which ought to have placed this in the centre of the composition and why

The château of Chaumont, aerial view.
The château of Chambord, aerial view.
(Air-photographer Roger Henrard.)

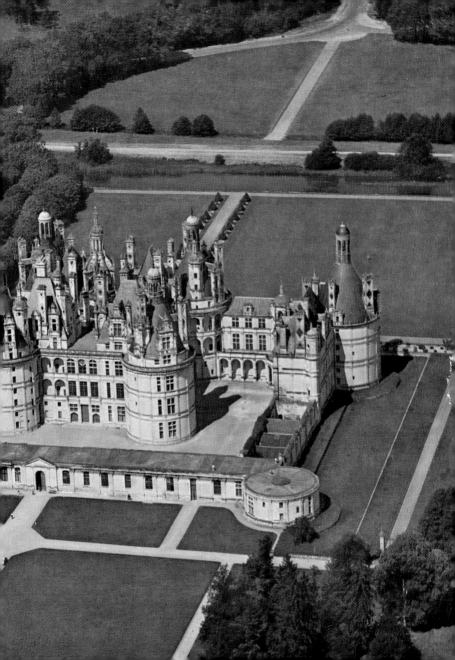

two towers of the fifteenth century were preserved, which should have been taken down.

At right angles to it is a second mass of buildings, of rather stern appearance, and which is characteristic of the Louis XIII style.

Inside, the large staircase, the guardrooms with beamed ceilings, the elegant chapel, bear witness to the wealth of the Brissac family. In 1620, Marie de Medici, after having escaped from Blois, had tempted to stir Anjou to revolt. It miscarried, following a bloodless combat at Ponts-de-Cé. And it was at Brissac that she was reconciled with her son.

The furniture is not lacking in interest, but one admires principally the beautiful tapestries.

The château now belongs to the twelfth duc de Brissac.

CHAMBORD

In the plain near the Cosson, in the centre of game forests, Chambord rises like a dream castle. Francis I was its instigator, wishing to own a residence worthy of his glory. Apparently he directed Domenico da Cortone to make a wooden model of it. However it was by French hands, those of Jacques and Denis Sourdeau, and Pierre Trinqueau, that Chambord was fashioned. The work was begun in 1519. The main walls were completed by 1533. But they worked on Chambord until the king's death.

The latter considered it as his home. Has he not, according to tradition, engraved on the glass of his study the famous distich :

> "Women often change
> Mad is he who trusts them ".

After the king's death, his successors from Henri II to Louis XIV continued to live at Chambord. The latter took the court there at various times (in 1669 and 1670). Molière's **Monsieur de Pourceaugnac** and the **Bourgeois Gentilhomme** were played there. The king had entrusted François Dorbay with important works, but the majority of them were never carried out. During the eighteenth century, the former King of Poland, Stanislas Leczinski, lived at Chambord between 1724 and 1733. The château was then given to Maurice de Saxe, who there trained a regiment of Uhlans and received his mistresses. It then passed to Polignac who established a stud-farm there. Napoléon I entrusted it to the Prince de Wagram. The Restoration presented it to the duc de Bordeaux, who took the title of comte de Chambord. Today it belongs to the State. The château, almost empty of furniture, contains some souvenirs of the Comte de Chambord and some coaches.

The plan of the château remains faithful to the structures of the Middle Ages. It is a huge rectangle flanked by large round towers at each angle, and completed, in the middle of one side by a monumental keep, which is itself flanked by round towers. In the centre of the

Chenonceaux, at night.
(Photographer Henry Paillasson.)

21

keep, at the intersection of four large guard rooms arranged as a greek cross, rises up the celebrated pierced staircase with its double spiral ramp. The guard rooms were formerly three floors high. They were cut down by coffered ceilings. The stair well was made in such a way that one can see from one ramp to the other, and it is crowned by a famous lantern 102 feet high.

But what is so extraordinary about Chambord is its superstructure. This stuns by the piling on of dormer windows, chimneys, spires, bell-turrets, capitals, which seem to spring up from the terraces, and, jumbled together, form the most sumptuous of ornaments, a decoration which one can see from afar; but near to, one can still admire this profusion, this richness. The lantern, alone, constitutes a masterpiece of technique and art : medallions, shells, pinnacles, all the decorative elements in fashion during the time of Francis I are here utilised.

Chambord, because of its architecture and its sculpture, is a subject which calls for special study. One can still see here signs of certain fifteenth century fortresses, at least in its general conception. The Italian influence manifests itself in the decoration, but it did not play any part in the elevation of the building. Nevertheless the builders did not fail to profit by the lesson which was offered them of the Francis I wing at Blois.

This château then is placed at a cross-roads of influences. One can criticize its gigantic proportions, its lack of harmony, but one must recognise its originality and the vast grandeur of its conception.

CHAUMONT

The château of Chaumont is admirably set in a wooded hillside, dominating the Loire : from afar, the large towers with their pepperpot roofs are caught sight of through the trees. Built on the border of Blésois and Touraine, it was one of those fortresses which protected a feudal frontier.

As a matter of fact one can find traces of a building of the Middle Ages. At first it belonged to the county of Blois, then passed to the Amboise family. In 1465 Pierre d'Amboise had the unfortunate idea of taking part in the war called "du Bien Public", a revolt of barons against the king their overlord : it was an unusual way of serving him. They were beaten. To punish the Lord of Chaumont, and to remove from him any desire to begin again, Louis XI gave orders for the citadel to be razed. He confiscated the château and dismantled it (1466). After which, like a good prince, he returned the land to its former owner.

Pierre undertook to rebuild the château. This work, commenced in 1466, was carried on by his son, Charles I of Amboise, the eldest of his seventeen children, and by his grandson Charles II, and was not finished until 1511.

The west wing and the north west tower were built after 1472, likewise the north wing, parallel to the Loire. The eastern and southern wings were built between 1498 and 1511 by Charles II. He was one of the better councillors of Louis XII. Courteously, he placed the arms of France and the initials of the king and Anne of Brittany on the two main buildings. One can see there also the coat of arms of George of Amboise who received the cardinal's hat at Chaumont in the presence of the king (1498).

In 1530, Catherine de Medici, widow of Henri II, acquired the château of Chaumont. She was soon to exchange it for Chenonceaux, with Diane de Poitiers, mistress of the dead king. Small revenge for a queen who was not ignorant of Diane's love for Chenonceaux.

Diane did not neglect Chaumont. She restored the wall-walk and signed the work with her initials interlaced with the arms attributed to the goddess after whom she was named : bows and quivers. The château afterwards passed to the La Marck family, to the duc de Beauvilliers, then to the Administrator of the Invalides, Le Ray, who settled in the outhouses the Italian potter, Nini.

Under the Empire, Chaumont was lived in by Mme. de Staël, exiled on Napoleon's orders. Today it is owned by the State.

It is still a feudal fortress. The entrance lies between two wings which date from the reign of Louis XII. It is flanked by two fat round pepperpot towers, girdled by a wall-walk and machicolations. The ground plan is a quadrilateral, but the northern wing, overlooking the Loire, was pulled down during the eighteenth century and the façades of the court underwent radical restoration in the course of the following century. Nevertheless one can see that, even if military elements are still extant, the sculptured decoration is very rich, the windows are numerous, and elegance takes the place of severity. On the ground floor a frieze which runs all along the façade is ornamented by mountains in flame : Chaud mont...

In the interior one visits the guard room, with its beautiful Beauvais tapestries, the council chamber hung with Flemish tapestries which are the work of Martin Reymbouts, and various rooms which are filled with Renaissance furniture.

At the entrance, a document room allows one to contemplate all the historical souvenirs which are connected with Chaumont. One can see there plans, old engravings, etc.

CHENONCEAUX

Chenonceaux in the Middle Ages was only a fortified manor house on the banks of the Cher, near a communal mill sitting in the middle of the river. The domain belonged to the de Marques family. The château was rebuilt by Jean II de Marques in 1411. Ruined, his heirs sold it in 1513 to Thomas Bohier, tax collector to Charles VIII, Louis XII and Francis I. Thomas determined to reconstruct the edifice, and Catherine Briçonnet, his wife, supervised the work while he accompanied the king to Italy. The old dungeon was retained, which received Italian decoration, and between 1515 and 1522, on the piles of the ancient mill was erected the elegant manor which holds its place as one of the masterpieces of the Renaissance.

Thomas Bohier died in 1524. In order to pay off his father's debts, and to humour the king, his son Antoine left the château to Francis I; Henri II in turn gave it to Diane de Poitiers. Philibert Delorme was ordered to throw a bridge over the Cher. Diane had beautiful gardens laid out at Chenonceaux. We have seen (cf. Chaumont) how, after the king's death, Catherine de Medici compelled Diane to exchange her château for Chaumont. The Queen built above the bridge the celebrated gallery on two floors, which gives Chenonceaux its originality. She organised dazzling fêtes of which Brantôme left a brilliant description.

At the end of the sixteenth century, the château passed to Louise de Lorraine, widow of Henri III, then to César de Vendôme. In 1730 the prince of Condé transferred it to the farmer-general Dupin, who received there Voltaire, Buffon, and Jean-Jacques Rousseau. It now belongs to the Menier family.

It is a country seat. Any military display has gone, and only the keep of the Marques, isolated on a terrace, recalls the ancient château. Overhanging turrets break the corners. The entrance is surmounted by a balcony supported by consoles. To the left lie the library and chapel, on the right the public rooms. The main building only comprises one floor above ground level over which magnificent dormer windows decorate the roof. The façade of the galleries already shows all the characteristics of classical architecture.

The interior formal staircase, like that at Azay-le-Rideau, gives access to a central vestibule from which rooms lead off. Diane's beautiful flowerbeds have been relaid with rare taste and help to give this home an aristocratic serenity, which was acknowledged by Flaubert.

25

25. Bellegarde.

BLOIS

26. La façade des loges.
The façade with the loggias.
Die Loggienfassade.

La facciata delle logge.
Fachada de los palcos.

BLOIS

28. L'oratoire. The oratory. Die Betkapelle. L'oratorio. Oratorio.

29. L'armoire aux poisons. The poison cupboard. Der Giftschrank. L'armadio dei veleni. Armario de los venenos.

30. Cour intérieure, aile Louis XII.
The inner court, Louis XII wing.
Innerer Hof, Flügel Ludwigs XII.
Cortile interno, ala Luigi XII.
Patio, ala de Luis XII.

31. L'escalier de l'aile François 1er.
Staircase of the Francis I wing.
Die Treppe und der Flügel Franz I.
Scala dell'ala Francesco I.
La escalera del ala de Francisco 1°.

32. Brissac.

33. Une chambre à coucher.
A bedroom.
Ein Schlafraum.
Una camera da letto.
Una alcoba.

CHAMBORD

34. Façade sur le Cosson.
Façade overlooking the Cosson.
Fassade auf den Cosson.

Facciata prospiciente il Cosson.
Fachada al Cosson.

CHAMBORD

35. La lanterne.
The lantern.
Die Laterne.
Il lucernario.
La linterna.

36. Sculptures sur les toits.
Sculptures on the roofs.
Dachskulpturen.
Sculture sui tetti.
Esculturas en el tejado.

37. Le grand escalier (à double rampe).
The great staircase.
Die große Doppeltreppe.
Scala monumentale a doppia rampa.
Escalera monumental (de doble barandilla).

CHAUMONT

38. Entrée du château.
The chateau entrance.
Schloßeingang.

Entrata del castello.
Entrada del castillo.

39. Puits de la cour in
rieure. A well in the in
court. Brunnen im Inn
hof. Pozzo del cor
interno. Pozo del pa
de honor.

Chenonceaux.

40. L'entrée. The
trance. Der Einga
L'ingresso. Entrada..

41. Le château sur
Cher. The chateau
the Cher. Das Sch
über dem Cher. Il cast
sul fiume Cher. El cast
sobre el Cher.

CHENONCEAUX

42

43

42. Cheverny.

43. Cheminée du grand salon, peinture de Mignard. Fireplace in the main drawing-room, a painting by Mignard. Kamin im großen Salon, Gemälde Mignards. Camino del salone. Il quadro è di Mignard. Chimenea del salón principal. Retrato por Mignard.

44. Chinon.

Le pavillon de l'horloge. The clock tower. Der Uhrtum. Padiglione dell'orologio. El pabellón del reloj.

45. La salle du trône.
The throne room.
Der Thronsaal.
Sala del trono.
El salón del Trono.

46. Tour de Boissy.
Boissy's tower.
Der Boissy-Turm.
Torre di Boissy.
La Torre de Boissy.

CHINON

47. **Tours et murailles.**
Towers and walls.
Türme und Mauern.
Torri e mura.
Torres y murallas.

FONTEVRAULT

**48. Toits des cuisines. Kitchen roofs. Dächer der Küchen.
Tetti delle cucine. Tejados de las cocinas.**

48

49

49. L'entrée du château. The chateau entrance. Schloß-eingang. L'entrata del castello. Entrada del castillo.

GIEN

50. L'église et le château. The church and chateau. Kirche und Schloß. Chiesa e castello. Iglesia y castillo.

51. La grande salle du château (Musée international de la chasse).
The great hall of the chateau (Hunting Museum).
Der große Saal (Jadgmuseum).
La sala grande del castello (Museo internazionale della caccia).
Salón del castillo (Museo internacional de caza).

Gien.

52-53. Musée de la chasse. Chaperon de faucon poires à poudre et cornes.

Museum : Falcon's Hood powder flasks and horns.

Jagdmuseum. Falkenkappe, Pulverblasen und Hörner.

Museo della caccia. Cappuccio di falco, fiaschetti per la polvere e corna.

Museo de caza caperuza de Halcón, cebadores y cuernas de pólvora.

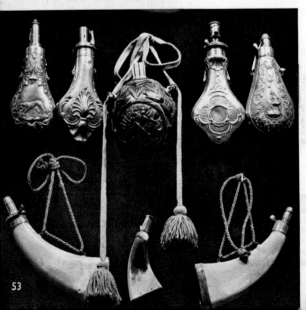

52

53

54. Langea

LANGEAIS

55

55. Façade sur les jardins.
Façade overlooking the gardens.
Gartenfassade.
La facciata sui giardini.
Fachada de los jardines.

CHEVERNY

The ancient château of Cheverny is only extant in two pavilions among the outhouses. The ground was acquired at the beginning of the sixteenth century by Jacques Hurault, of a family faithful to the monarchy. His son Raoul, was President of the **Chambre des Comptes,** his grandson was Chancellor of France. It was the latter's son, Henri, who built the present château, finished in 1634.

An example of the Louis XIII style, Cheverny is simple in layout. The main central section, three floors high, is flanked by less elevated wings which end with two pavilions roofed by quadrangular domes of massive aspect, themselves crowned by lanterns. The windows are surmounted by pediments. On the main façade twelve niches separate the first floor windows and they shelter busts. The horizontal bands of stone do not break the monotony and frigidity of this façade.

The interior retains its furniture intact and is perhaps the most complete collection of this epoch that can be seen in France. In the king's room, under a coffered ceiling, elegant woodwork is adorned by little painted panels, the work of the Blois artist Jean Mosnier, whom we have already met at Beauregard. They represent allegorical scenes taken from romances of that time. In the guard room, a magnificent tapestry from a Parisian workshop is consecrated to the history of Ulysses. It was woven after the cartoons of Simon Vouet. One comes across Jean Mosnier again in a neighbouring room in which he painted the adventures of Don Quixote.

One of Cheverny's charms is found in the magnificent park which surrounds the château. This park, where woods and sheets of water merge to make an admirable composition, has undergone a few transformations. Grass swards had replaced flowerbeds in the French seventeenth century style, which are now being restored.

But Cheverny is not a home settled in the past. The château belongs to the Marquis de Vibraye, a descendant of the Hurault family, and is still lived in. And the huntsmen, at the end of a day's chase sound the "Death" there as they did in the time of Henri de Cheverny.

CHINON

Chinon's defensive wall broken by towers and its vigorous curtain wall stretch along an admirable site above the Vienne. But now it is no more than a stone skeleton arising from the green hill. But so thrilling is its history, that one willingly overlooks the ruined state of this mediaeval fortress. Intimately involved in the struggle between Capetians and Plantagenets, it saw the death of Henry II and his son Richard the Lionheart. Philippe Auguste took possession of it in 1205 after a year's siege. The dauphin Charles, driven from Paris, found security there, where he received Joan of Arc in March 1429. When king, Charles VII continued to live at Chinon until 1449. All his successors, until Louis XII, resided there also. Passing into the hands of Cardinal Richelieu, the château was badly maintained. The Cardinal had no love for citadels of the Middle Ages. Under the First Empire the château served as a quarry and saltpetre factory. Acquired by the Department of Indre-et-Loire, it was restored with care after 1855 by the initiative of Mérimée, Inspector of Historical Monuments.

Built on the site of an ancient gallo-roman fortified town, the citadel consists of three castles separated by moats. To the east rises the Fortress of Saint George, built for Henry II. Only the ruins of the crypt and the chapel remain.

The central château. One reaches it by passing under the clock tower, a high elongated tower so-named because it holds a bell which chimed the hours. In it has recently been installed an interesting museum devoted to Joan of Arc. Various towers flank the rectangular enclosure on the south side of which were found the royal apartments. One can still see the remains of the great hall where Charles VII received Joan.

It was in the **Château de Coudray,** joined to the latter by a bridge, that Joan of Arc stayed. The Coudray tower was built by Philippe Auguste, and is a remarkable military work. There were locked up, in dungeons which still bear traces of graffiti which they scrawled, the dignitaries of the order of the Temple, among whom was Jacques de Molay, their grandmaster.

The charming town of Chinon is rich in beautiful monuments. The church of Saint-Maurice, the church of Saint-Etienne (finished in 1477 by Philippe de Commines) the Grand Carroi and the rue Voltaire with their half-timbered houses and ancient mansions. At Chinon, memories of Joan of Arc are mingled with those of Rabelais.

FOUGÈRES

The château of Fougères-sur-Bièvre, situated about 15 miles south of Blois, was built by Pierre de Refuge, treasurer to King Louis XI, and by his son-in-law, Jean de Villefresne. It was built in 1470 and replaced a more ancient fortress.

Nevertheless it is still a mediaeval work, the same type of castle which was erected during the second half of the fifteenth century, before the advent of new forms brought from Italy. The structure is disposed around one courtyard in a trapezoid form. The entrance is surmounted by two turrets. A passage supported by flattened arches communicates with a square keep and a round tower. An elegant arcaded gallery equally squat, crowned by elegant high roofed attic windows, recalls the gallery built at Blois by Charles d'Orléans.

The doors are decorated with basket-handle arches and sculptures. During the sixteenth century numerous windows were made to give the rooms more light and grace. These also still contain some beautiful sculptured fireplaces.

GIEN

An important crossing place on the Loire, Gien was at an early age a fortified town. The château itself, in its entirety, was the work of Anne de Beaujeu, daughter of Louis XI and Regent during the minority of her brother, the future Charles VIII. Anne, who married Pierre de Bourbon, seigneur de Beaujeu, received the county of Gien on her marriage. She looked after the town with care, which knew two centuries of great prosperity. Mansions, houses, convents multiplied. It was at Gien where, under the Fronde, the adolescent Louis XIV took refuge, together with Mazarin and Anne of Austria, in 1652.

During the eighteenth century, the manufacture of earthenware contributed to maintain the town's prosperity and everywhere made its fame. Gien suffered badly during the second World War and lost, in the course of bombing and fire many witnesses of its past. The town was reconstructed with taste, and the architects, without imitating, knew how to give back to the city its original character by using principally local material.

By luck, the château was practically undamaged and retained its original appearance. Built in 1484, that is to say the extreme end of the fifteenth century, it seems less like a military stronghold than a country seat. What constitutes the originality of this château is the use that has been made of its red and black bricks. It seems that Anne de Beaujeu, preoccupied by economy, tried to adorn the château mainly by decorative designs in the form of lozenges chequers, circles, herring-bones, or fish nets. The structure is composed of two parts set at right angles. Towards the Loire, the main building is flanked on one side by a small square tower, at the other by a round one. On the interior promenade, a polygonal stair-tower, is entered by a door crowned by a four-centered arch, above which is a square room supported by corbelling. Elegant small towers flank the other wing.

Since 1952, the château has housed the International Museum of Hunting where remarkable collections of arms, engravings, tapestries and paintings, amongst which is a fine collection of paintings by François Desportes (1661-1743), illustrate with rare taste the evolution of hunting and the arts which it has inspired.

The Museum was enriched in 1792 by an exceptional collection of trophies belonging to Claude Hettier de Boislambert, accumulated throughout fifty years of hunting all over the world. This collection interests hunters and non-hunters alike and receives thousands of visitors each year.

LANGEAIS

At the border of Touraine and Anjou, Count Foulque Nerra built at the end of the tenth century a square keep which is considered one of the oldest in France. One can see the ruins almost overgrown which rise up at a little distance from the new château.

Langeais was for long contested. Richard the Lionheart seized it at the end of the twelfth century but Philippe Auguste secured it again before long. During the Hundred Years War the English garrisoned it, but were soon dislodged. The fortress was in a pitiful state when Louis XI gave it to Jean Bourré, treasurer of Finances, and invited him to entirely reconstruct the citadel. The Duke of Brittany, still independant, was making bold to menace the kingdom by forming an alliance with the king's enemies, and in particular the Duke of Burgundy. It was necessary to bar his passage should the occasion arise.

Thus it is still a castle which Jean Bourré erected. It was completed in 1467 and was never used as a fortress. The marriage of Charles VIII and Anne of Britanny celebrated at Langeais on 16th December 1491 put a stop to feudal wrangles.

Nevertheless Langeais retains the forbidding aspect of a stronghold. The windows are narrow and placed high up. The wall are high and thick. The wall-walk encircles the château. The drawbridge is flanked by two huge towers. The moats, which it was necessary to cross, are now filled in ; the keep, built into the main façade, only communicates by the wall-walk with the main apartments.

These lie at right angles. The interior façade is less austere. But the superposed windows are still small, broken by mullions. Two hexagonal towers contain spiral staircases.

Langeais was acquired during the nineteenth century by M. Siegfried who bequeathed it to the Institut de France after having installed magnificent furnishings there. One admires the beautiful tapestries (some of which originated at the Château of Plessis-Macé) the furniture, and ancient works of art. The room where the marriage of Anne and Charles VIII took place has been restored. Beautiful flowerbeds in the French style stretch out in front of the southern façade.

LOCHES

Like the citadel of Chinon, the château of Loches was at first a vast fortified enclosure which was bitterly fought for by Capetians and Plantagenets. Philippe Auguste seized it, during the captivity of Richard the Lionheart in 1193, with the complicity of John Lackland. Once free, Richard took it by surprise. But in the course of his victorious campaigns, Philippe Auguste recovered it after a long siege. Loches has never ceased to belong to the royal domain, and since the fifteenth century has served as a state prison. Under Charles VII, Agnes Sorel, Mlle de Beauté, resided in the royal apartments. Louis XI confined there those who ceased to please him. Cardinal Balue experienced the cruel severity of the king's "**fillettes**", uncomfortable wooden cages. Later, Ludovic Sforza, Duke of Milan, taken prisoner by Louis XII at the Battle of Novara, was an inmate of its dungeons.

The most ancient part of the château is its keep, a powerful square mass built at the extremity of a hill and the promontory which is an extension of it. It was constructed by the count of Anjou, Geoffroy Martel, at the end of the eleventh century. The strong walls are supported by cylindrical buttresses. During the fifteenth century the keep was much dilapidated, the enclosure, already protected by beak-shaped towers was reinforced by an entrance pavilion with a drawbridge, the Martelet and New Tower. It was in this latter that Cardinal Balue was incarcerated. One can still see there instruments of torture of uncertain application.

In the Martelet, which contains three floors of dungeons, Ludovic Sforza decorated his prison with curious frescoes.

The strength of this fortress contrasts with the grace of the Royal Apartments in the façade dominating the Indre and the town. Nevertheless the first main buildings, of the fourteenth century, retain their severe appearance, and the wall-walk is flanked with little towers. At the end, the tower called **La Belle Agnès** contains the tomb of Agnès Sorel, a nobly treated recumbant figure, the work of Jacques Morel. It was placed there by the General-prefet Pommereul. The new château, built under Louis XII is architecturally gracious, and the oratory of Anne of Brittany is in the flamboyant gothic style.

Between the mediaeval fortress and the Royal Apartments the collegial church of Saint-Ours, of the end of the twelfth century, has a nave covered by hollow pyramids.

With regard to the town of Loches, it is rich in monuments, amongst which one must at least see the Picoys Gate, the Town Hall, the Chancellery, or Hotel Nau, the Saint-Antoine Tower, etc.

LE LUDE

Le Lude only half belongs to the Loire valley. It in fact rises up on the borders of Anjou and Maine. But, as with Châteaudun, it is on the road to the châteaux, and visitors are well-advised to make a detour to see it and at the same time be present at the nocturnal spectacle which takes place there in summer.

It is a Renaissance building but lacks homogeneity. The powerful Lords of Daillon, who owned the land, undertook its construction towards the end of the fifteenth century and to that epoch belongs the north wing. The south wing and the interior façades were built during the sixteenth century. The medallions which decorate the walls, the line of mouldings which separate the floors, are very characteristic. The eastern wing was not finished until the end of the eighteenth century.

Inside, the royal apartments are adorned with beautiful tapestries. Some interesting frescoes were discovered on the ground floor in 1833. The park is encircled by the lazy waters of the Loir.

LUYNES

This sturdy feudal fortress dominates the Loire. It was transformed in the second half of the fifteenth century by Hardouin de Maillé who constructed a home of brick and stone, similar to the neighbouring manor of Plessis-lez-Tours. In the seventeenth century a wing in the classical style completed the work.

Charles d'Albert, councillor and minister of Louis XIII was rewarded for his good and loyal services by his land being converted into a duchy, and the village henceforth took the name of its owner.

The four massive towers of the château overlook some of the most beautiful scenery in the valley.

MÉNARS

Situated upstream from Blois, on the right bank of the Loire, Ménars is a sober building of the seventeenth century (1646). In 1760 it was acquired by the Marquise de Pompadour who spent much time there and sometimes considered retiring there altogether. The château was enlarged and surrounded by a spacious park. On the death of the Marquise, it passed to her brother Abel de Marigny (Minister of Works) who carried on the work with the help of Gabriel and Soufflot. Marshal Victor, then the Prince de Chimay and their descendants owned Ménars in turn.

The park is magnificent. One reaches the terrace by a double flight of steps; the low walls on each side end with griffins of female form, one of which was modelled from that of the Marquise's own bosom. A colonnaded grotto, the work of Soufflot, is placed below the terrace. Gardens stretch down as far as the river. They are embellished by flowerbeds, vases and a Temple of Venus.

The château itself consists of a block of buildings set back between two projecting parts; the first floor is topped by a high roof pierced by dormer windows.

MONTGEOFFROY

Of the château built by the de la Grandière family, to the east of Angers, all that remains are two round towers and a chapel in the flamboyant style. The property was acquired at the end of the eighteenth century by Marshal de Contades, one of the military leaders of Louis XV reign, and governor of Alsace. Contades took on the Parisian architect Barré, who from 1773 onwards built the main rectangular mass, flanked at both ends by wings at right angles. A pediment crowns the central pavilion which slightly projects from the rest of the façade. This is sober and balanced, topped by high slate roofs.

Marshal de Contades furnished Montgeoffroy luxuriously. Paintings and Flemish tapestries decorate the walls. The suites of furniture remain untouched and are still in the position the marshal placed them in. The property in fact still belongs to his descendants. The château is an excellent example of French provincial architecture of the reign of Louis XVI.

The rooms contain canvases by Poussin, Van Loo, and Desportes. One cannot but admire in the great drawing-room the delicious portrait of a young child in fancy dress. It is the work of Drouais, and the model is none other than the young Hérault de Séchelles, future member of the Convention, and later to be guillotined, whose mother, it is said, had a weakness for Marshal de Contades.

MONTRÉSOR

The château is situated on a slight rise above the Indrois, north-east of Loches. Among the trees, one sees the remains of the mediaeval fortress with its untopped round towers. The first château of Montrésor was naturally built by Foulque Nerra.

That which one visits to-day dates only from the first years of the sixteenth century. It is the work of Imbert de Bastarnay. The gracious manorial buildings have five large mullioned windows on each floor and attic windows still decorated with crocketed pinnacles. Round towers stand at each end.

The château of Montrésor was restored during the last century by a descendant of a great Polish family, which is why it contains works of art, pictures and souvenirs of that country.

The church, somewhat more recent than the château, is a Renaissance building (1520-61) : one can see there beautiful stained glass in the apse, the stalls, and particularly the tomb of the Bastarnay family.

MONTREUIL-BELLAY

Bellay, Lord of Montreuil, gave his name to this little town south of Saumur. The first château was erected at the beginning of the eleventh century by Foulque Nerra. Rebuilt two centuries later, it was transformed and completed during the fourteenth and fifteenth centuries by Guillaume d'Harcourt.

The "Château-Vieux" faces south and forms a right angle with the little château, an elegant work of the fifteenth century where were entertained the Canons in charge of the ancient chapel (today the Church of Notre-Dame). It also contains a beautiful kitchen of the Middle Ages. The "Château-Neuf", more imposing, has its doors decorated with sculptured motives and its windows mullioned. But the pepper-pot roofs have been replaced by terraces easier to protect against canon balls. One finds inside an oratory decorated with frescoes, beautiful furniture, tapestries, etc.

Montreuil-Bellay at the end of the last century belonged to a vine-grower named Nivelleau who may have served Balzac as a model, when he wrote of old Grandet in the famous novel.

MONTSOREAU

On the borders of Anjou and Touraine, near the little port of Rest which was used by the nuns of Fontevrault, the château is a fifteenth century building, improved and embellished in the following century. Replacing a more ancient building, it was built towards 1440 by Jean de Chambes, steward to Charles VII. The façade on the Loire, which flows at its feet, is still severe. Nevertheless in the upper part, the attic windows on two floors with the ramparts of the gables with foliated finials and sculpted pinnacles bear witness to a decorative refinement which bursts out with more exuberance in the inner court and the full height of the elegant little stair tower erected towards 1530. Amusing low-reliefs decorate this tower between each window.

Charles de Chambes, a descendant of the builder, and Françoise de Maridor, were the heroes of a drama evoked by Alexandre Dumas. But the assassination of Bussy d'Amboise in fact took place at la Coutancière, some leagues to the north, on the other bank of the Loire.

After belonging to the de Sourches family the property was broken up after the Revolution. Acquired by the Department of Maine-et-Loire it was the object of felicitous restoration. A few years ago the Goum (1) Museum was placed there.

(1) An Algerian Regiment.

56. Loches. The Keep.

57. Le château et l'église Saint-Ours.
The chateau and the church of Saint-Ours.
Schloß und Saint-Ours-Kirche.
Il castello e la chiesa di Saint-Ours.
Castillo e iglesia de Saint-Ours.

58. Tombeau d'Agnès Sorel.
The tomb of Agnes Sorel.
Grabmal der Agnes Sorel.
Tomba di Agnès Sorel.
Sepulcro de Inès Sorel.

LE LUDE

59. **Le Lude, la nuit.**
    At night.
    Nacht.
    Veduta di notte.
    De noche.

60. **Luyn**

MÉNARS

61. Les jardins.
The gardens.
Die Gärten.
I giardini.
Jardines.

62. Façade d'entrée.
Entrance façade.
Fassade des Eingangs.
La facciata d'ingresso.
Fachada de la entrada.

61

62

63. La cuisine. The kitchen. Die Küche. La cucina. La cocina.

65. Montrésor.

66. La porte principale.
The main gateway.
Die Hauptpforte.
La porta principale.
Puerta principal.

MONTREUIL-BELLAY

67. Montreuil-Bellay.   68. Montsoreau.

69. Orléans.
Tours de la cathédrale.
Cathedral towers.
Türme der Kathedrale.
Le torri della cattedrale.
Torres de la catedral.

70. Le Plessis-Bourré.
La façade du château.
The chateau façade.
Schloßfassade.
La facciata del castello.
Fachada del castillo.

71. Le Plessis-Macé.

72. Saun

73. Saumur et la Loire. Saumur and the Loire. Saumur mit der Loire.

Saumur e la Loira. Saumur y el Loire.

74. Serrant.

75. Portail d'entrée.
Entrance gate.
Eingangsportal.
Portale d'ingresso.
Verja de entrada.

77. Talcy.

78. Perron dans le parc.
Steps in the park.
Treppe im Park.
Scalinata nel parco.
Escalinata en el parque.

78

79. Tours.
Musée des Beaux-Arts et tours de la cathédrale.
Art Gallery and towers of the cathedral.
Kunstmuseum und Türme der Kathedrale.
Museo delle Belle Arti e torri della cattedrale.
Museo de Bellas Artes y torres de la catedral.

80. Ussé vu des bords de l'Indre.
Ussé seen from the banks of the Indre.
Ussé von den Ufern des Indre aus.
Ussé visto dalle rive dell'Indre.
Vista de Ussé desde las orillas del Indre.

81. Le donjon et le parc.
The keep and the park.
Wachtturm und Park.
Il mastio ed il parco.
Torre del homenaje y parque.

82. La cour.
The courtyard.
Der Hof.
Il cortile.
Patio.

83. Une chambre à coucher.
A bedroom.
Ein Schlafraum.
Una camera da letto.
Une alcoba.

84. Valençay, la nuit.
At night.
Nacht.
Veduta di notte.
De noche.

LE PLESSIS-BOURRÉ

Long inaccessible to the public, this château situated 10 miles north of Angers is one of the most beautiful in the region. In 1462 Jean Bourré, financial secretary to Louis XI, whom we have already met at Langeais, bought the property of Plessis-au-Vent. He at once undertook the erection of a huge château structurally recalling that of Langeais.

Surrounding it is a wide moat which today forms an admirable mirror of water in which is reflected the whiteness of Angevin rock. The château is rectangular with large towers at each corner. The improvement of the defenses, by the creation of an exterior terrace which encircles the building and facilitates grazing fire, permits the lowering of the wings while retaining the height of the main bulk of buildings. Facing the bridge, the entrance is still well protected. The south-east tower, with its machicolations, plays the role of keep; that at the north-east contains the chapel.

Inside, the guard-room is covered by a partitioned wooden roof. An artist of great talent has decorated this with little allegorical scenes illustrating proverbs or old fables. All the gallic verve of their native forbears is given free reign in these vigorous compositions.

LE PLESSIS-MACÉ

This other Plessis, situated north-west of Angers, was given its name by one of its foremost seigneurs: Mathieu or Macé. The keep of the twelfth century, restored and strengthened in the fifteenth century, lifts up its bare walls in the middle of brambles and vegetation. It rests against an enclosure broken by towers.

In the fifteenth century, the de Beaumont family built a comfortable L-shaped building, at the angle of which an exterior balcony gives an original appearance. The dormer windows are decorated by sharply-pointed gables. At the end of one of the wings, the chapel, in the flamboyant gothic style, contains woodwork carved with rare delicacy.

The XXth century saw the restoration of the window leading, the pavement and the walls of the chapel, but not that of the building itself which retains its elegant character and one understands why various French kings, from Louis XI to Henry IV, slept there. One should not neglect casting an eye on the outhouses. One tall barn built like an upturned ship's hull allows one to gauge the importance of this ancient manor.

SAUMUR

The château of Saumur was erected in the eleventh century to defend the eastern border of Anjou against the depredations of the Counts of Blois. It was a stake in the struggle between the Plantagenets and the Capetians, and became part of the royal estates during the reign of Philippe Auguste. It was never taken by the English, during the Hundred Years War.

The existing château was completely rebuilt by Louis I of Anjou at the end of the fourteenth century and finished by Louis II, his son. It is reproduced in one of the miniatures of the **Très Riches Heures** of the Duc de Berry, just as it appears, very white above the Loire, dominating the city, the steeple of the church of Saint-Pierre and the belfry of the Town Hall. And yet it has undergone numerous modifications. In the fifteenth century, King René, who enjoyed living in Saumur, embellished it. In the sixteenth century, it served as a Huguenot stronghold and Duplessis-Mornay, who was its governor, increased the defenses and altered those existing to strengthen them. During the seventeenth century, as with many Loire châteaux, it became a state prison. There were sent noble youths imprisoned upon receiving **lettres de cachet.** They were not too unhappy there. Appropriated by the army in the nineteenth century, it was acquired by the town of Saumur in 1906 and restored with care by the Administrators of Historic Monuments. It needed it.

All the superstructures, the bell turrets, weathervanes, chimneys and ornamental ridges, which King René so much admired, have disappeared. They were replaced by pepperpot or conical roofs. The south-west wing, already in a bad state of repair in the eighteenth century, was pulled down and replaced by a terrace. Indeed the ground plan was formerly a quadrilateral. Each wing is flanked by towers round at their base and octogonal at their summit, reinforced by slender buttresses and crowned by trefoil machicolations. The mullioned windows open onto the inner courtyard. The ornamentation is very elaborate in the higher parts. It is mainly concentrated on the stair-turret.

Inside, one visits the Museum of Religious Art, arranged with exquisite taste (wood carvings, liturgical ornaments, works of art, etc.), the Museum of Decorative Art, with a collection of earthenware and porcelain (the Lair Collection), beautiful tapestries, Limoges enamels and some furniture and paintings. One likewise should visit the original Riding Museum which certainly has its place in Saumur.

SERRANT

It is both the most oriental and the latest of the Renaissance châteaux. In fact although it was begun in the sixteenth century after the designs of the architect Philibert Delorme, it was not finished until the eighteenth century. Its building was undertaken by Charles de Brie towards 1546. Ruined following a law-suit, the family of de Brie sold Serrant in 1596 to the duke de Montbazon who forty years later made it over to Guillaume Bautru, councillor and servant of Louis XIII and

Richelieu. Bautru heightened the château — which then only comprised a ground and first floor — with a higher floor of ungainly appearance. He received Louis XIV at Serrant. His son-in-law, the Marquis de Vaubrun, was killed in the battle of Altenheim, and to receive the remains of her husband, Bautru's daughter prolonged the southern wing and had built by Hardoin-Mansart the chapel which contains a fine funeral monument, the work of Coysevox. For the sake of symmetry, the northern wing was lengthened in the eighteenth century.

The property of Serrant belonged before the Revolution to the family of de Walsh. Lady-in-waiting to the Empress, Countess Walsh organised a reception in honour of Napoleon and Josephine, who stayed there in 1808, and that is why one finds inside furniture in the Empire style.

Facing the gardens, admirably laid out, two large towers flank the façade and are reflected in a sheet of water.

SULLY

Sully owes its existence to its position. The château defended a crossing of the Loire east of Orléans. The possession of George de la Trémoille, the favourite of the dauphin Charles, it received Joan of Arc and the King shortly before the coronation at Reims. Acquired by Maximilien de Béthune for 333,00 **livres** in 1602 the estate was raised to a duchy by Henri IV, wishing to reward his servant. Sully, who was to write **Royal Economies** at the château, embellished it and above all transformed the park and its approaches. Louis XIV and Anne of Austria stayed there during the Fronde. Sully was used as a residence by Voltaire, exiled from Paris by the Regent for having expressed himself too caustically in his writings. The château suffered badly from bombing in 1940 and 1944. Its restoration is being completed.

The château, whose foundations were formerly washed by the Loire but are now separated from it by an embankment, is surrounded by deep moats and goes back to the beginning of the fifteenth century. This mediaeval fortress was designed in plan as an irregular trapezium. The buildings to the north form the keep. It has towers at each corner. It was in one of its great halls that Voltaire had comedies performed. Above, one admires the magnificent old timbers. The eastern façade, with its wall-walk is of less forbidding appearance.

TALCY

On the borders of Beauce, to the north of Blois, the château of Talcy, which belongs to the State, has undergone little restoration during the nineteenth century (except for a few windows to light it better). It dates, as a whole, from the first quarter of the sixteenth century. It was built in fact about 1520 by a rich Florentine banker,

Bernard Salviati, related to Catherine de Medici. It is however possible that Salviati was content only to reinforce the defenses of a fortress built in the fifteenth century, for the château is still very mediaeval in appearance and the interior gallery recalls that of Charles d'Orléans at Blois.

The postern opens under the keep which is flanked by three little turrets joined together by a wall-walk. The main buildings, set at right angles, comprise a wing with a gallery topped by two crocketted gables, and another wing of a more restrained design altered under Louis XIII.

Bernard Salviati was the father of Cassandre, whose praises Ronsard sung, and grandfather of Diane, Agrippa d'Aubigné's beloved. Talcy served as a setting for an interview (which did not achieve success) between Catherine de Medici and Charles IX, the King of Navarre, and Condé (1562) to restore peace to the Kingdom of France.

Its furnishing, ill-assorted enough, includes Renaissance pieces, panelling, seventeenth century tapestries and some Louis XV furniture. The pigeon house, of great age, is remarkably preserved.

USSÉ

Not far from the Indre, Ussé hides in the forest between Tours and Chinon. It is a magnificent château, which, like Chaumont, was laid out as quadrilateral, until the time when, in the seventeenth century, one of its sides was thrown down to open up the view over the valley. The exterior façades, contemporary with Langeais, are imposing, with their defensive display of towers and wall-walks. Nevertheless they are already wide open to air and light while the interior façades are adorned with Renaissance grace. They were finished about 1520. The château was fully completed in 1557. The classical style is already noticeable there.

The estate belonged to the de Bueil family. It was Jean V and his son Antoine who built the château. It then passed to the d'Espinay family, responsible for the Renaissance parts, and the chapel. In the seventeenth century, Ussé belonged to Thomas Bernin, whose son knocked down the north wing, and whose grandson married Vauban's daughter. The duke de Rohan-Montbazon, then the Duchess de Duras, were successively the proprietors of Ussé, which today is owned by the de Blacas family.

The chapel, built between 1521 and 1528 by Charles d'Espinay, is a remarkable building in the Renaissance style.

VALENÇAY

It really is not quite fair to connect Valençay, which is in Berry, with the Loire châteaux, but its architects have borrowed elements

86. Façade principale.
The main façade.
Hauptfassade.
Facciata principale.
Fachada principal.

Villandry, la nuit.
At night.
Nacht.
Veduta di notte.
De noche.

87. Les douves et le château.
The moat and the chateau.
Die Gräben und das Schloß.
I fossati ed il castello.
Las cavas y castillo.

88. Les jardins. The gardens. Die Gärten. I giardini. Sus jardines.

from Chambord and Chenonceaux. Thus Valençay still belongs to the valley, or more exactly, to its tributaries.

Jacques d'Etampes, who built it towards 1540, aimed too high. He was only able to finish the north wing which includes the great central pavilion, the keep and two towers, covered by domes. A lantern turret caps them. The antique orders are superimposed. The Renaissance triumphs at Valençay, and the Classical style is proclaimed.

A right-angled western wing was built by the great grandson of Jacques d'Etampes in the middle of the seventeenth century. It was modified after 1770 by a new owner, the farmer-general Legendre, who finished off the work with the New Tower.

The Prince de Talleyrand, occupier of Valençay, left numerous and magnificent souvenirs of his stay in this noble building.

VILLANDRY

One comes above all to Villandry on account of the celebrated gardens which embellish the château ; but the building itself is very interesting. It is composed of three main buildings framing the court of honour. The western wing ends towards the south with a huge square keep of the twelfth century, all that remains of the earlier work. The château was built about 1532 for Jean Le Breton, secretary of State to Francis I, who watched the erection of Chambord. During the eighteenth century, Villandry belonged to the de Castellane family. One is indebted to Dr. Carvallo, whose heirs continue to own the château, for its restoration and for the gardens.

The building, supported by a terrace, shows all the characteristics of the Renaissance : pilasters surround the windows, wide mouldings separate the ground and first floor, mullioned dormer windows are topped by sculptured gables, flanked with pinnacles...

Inside is preserved an important collection of paintings mainly of the Venetian and Spanish schools.

The grounds are famous. They show the layout of sixteenth century gardens, with their three superimposed stages ; water-garden, ornamental garden and vegetable garden. Springs and fountains animate the mirrors of the ornamental lakes. In the pleasure garden, clumps of box form elegant geometrical motives which enhance the symmetry of yew. Even the arrangement of the vegetables in the third garden makes a cleverly coloured pattern. At night, with flood-lighting, the gardens of Villandry take on new tints and glitter in the darkness.

Printed off on 20 June 1975
by SCOP-SADAG, Bellegarde.
The first edition of this book was published in 1962.
The " Dépôt légal " was made first quarter 1962.
Publisher number 875 — Printer number 1172

© Arthaud 1975. Printed in France
S B N 2 - 7003 - 0091 - 2